JAMS, JELLIES &
PRESERVES

Consultant Editor:
Valerie Ferguson

LORENZ BOOKS

Contents

Introduction

Fresh produce can be preserved in a variety of ways giving you delicious, and often economical, jams, jellies, preserves and chutneys the whole year through. Making jams and jellies is the perfect way to deal with a glut of fruit and they have an intensity of flavour rare in commercial varieties. Do not overlook savoury jellies, as they will add piquancy to simple meat dishes. Jams contain whole fruits or pieces of fruit, while jellies are made from the strained liquid produced during the initial cooking of the fruit.

Windfall and end-of-season fruit makes good chutney, but always choose good-quality, unbruised fruit for bottling. As a general rule, when bottling fruit, the syrup should just cover the surface.

Home-made candied fruit, so much better than purchased mixed peel, is best made in late winter when the new season's citrus fruit is available.

Pickles, chutneys and relishes are piquant and easy to make. Always use stainless steel or enamelled pans that will not react with the vinegar or the acid in the vegetables and fruit.

Don't forget to make extra quantities, as jams and preserves make excellent and much appreciated gifts!

Techniques

Choosing Containers

Glass jars and bottles are a popular choice for all kinds of preserves because they are durable, versatile and decorative, enhancing the appearance of their contents. Modern recycled glass has many of the qualities of antique glass, such as flaws and colourings, and is inexpensive.

Earthenware jars and pots are also good choices for chutneys and home-made mustards. Specially made preserving jars are best for bottled fruit and vegetables and can be reused, although you should always use fresh seals.

Sterilizing

To ensure that harmful bacteria are eliminated, it is essential to sterilize bottles and jars and their lids, if they have them. This can be done in a variety of ways. To sterilize in the oven, stand the containers on a baking sheet lined with newspaper or on a wooden board and rest their lids on them, but do not seal. It is important to make sure they are not touching. Place them in a cold oven and then turn it on to 110°C/225°F/Gas ¼ and leave the containers for in the oven for 30 minutes.

This method has the advantage of ensuring the containers are warm when they are filled with hot jam, syrup or chutney; otherwise they would crack. If you are not going to use the sterilized containers immediately, cover them with a clean cloth and make sure they are warmed again before being filled.

An alternative method is to put the containers and their lids in an empty dishwasher and run it on its hottest setting, including the drying cycle, but without adding any detergent. This, too, will ensure that the containers are warm when they are filled.

It is also necessary to sterilize a jelly bag before use. Set the bag over a large bowl and carefully pour boiling water through it. Discard the water and replace the bowl with a clean one. The jelly bag is now ready to use.

Seals and Labels

The type and effectiveness of the seal required depend on the kind of preserve and the process used. Jams and jellies can be covered with a disc of greaseproof (waxed) paper and the top of the jar covered with paper or cellophane held in place with an elastic band. Bottled fruit and vegetables must be sealed with new rubber seals and the lids clipped in place. Chutneys and pickles that are preserved in vinegar should be sealed with vinegar-proof lids that will not corrode.

Ideally, all preserves should be labelled with a description of the contents and the date they were made. Self-adhesive labels may be attached to the surface of the container or wooden or metal labels may be tied around the neck.

Setting Point

To test jams and jellies for the setting point, spoon a small quantity on to a chilled saucer. Chill for 3 minutes, then push the jam with your finger. If wrinkles form on the surface, the jam is ready. Alternatively, you could use a sugar thermometer clipped to the side of the pan, but not touching the base. When the temperature reaches 105°C/ 220°F, the jam is ready.

Most jams will benefit if left to stand for about 15 minutes before being ladled into jars. This ensures that the pieces of fruit are evenly distributed. A jam funnel is useful for preventing hot spillages; it can also be used when filling jars with chutney.

Strawberry Jam

Capture the essence of summer in a jar of home-made strawberry jam – perfect to serve with scones and clotted cream.

Makes about 1.5 kg/3 lb

INGREDIENTS
1 kg/2¼ lb/8 cups small strawberries
900 g/2 lb/4½ cups granulated (white)
    sugar
juice of 2 lemons

1 Place the strawberries in layers in a large bowl, sprinkling each layer with sugar. Cover and leave overnight.

2 The next day, scrape the fruit and juice into a large, heavy-based pan. Add the lemon juice. Gradually bring to the boil over a low heat, stirring until the sugar has dissolved.

COOK'S TIPS: For best results, don't wash the strawberries. Instead, carefully brush off any dirt, or wipe the strawberries with a damp cloth. If you have to wash any pieces of fruit, pat them dry and then spread them out on a clean dish towel to dry further. This strawberry jam can be stored in a cool, dark place for up to 1 year.

3 Boil steadily for 10–15 minutes, or until the jam reaches setting point. Cool for 10 minutes.

4 Pour the jam into warm sterilized jars, filling them right to the top. Cover and seal the jars while hot and label when cold.

Rhubarb & Ginger Mint Jam

Ginger mint is easily grown in the garden, and is just the thing to boost the flavour of rhubarb jam.

Makes about 2.75 kg/6 lb

INGREDIENTS
2 kg/4½ lb rhubarb, trimmed
250 ml/8 fl oz/1 cup water
juice of 1 lemon
5 cm/2 in piece fresh root
    ginger
1.5 kg/3 lb/6¾ cups granulated (white) sugar
115 g/4 oz/⅔ cup preserved stem
    ginger, chopped
30–45 ml/2–3 tbsp very finely chopped
    ginger mint leaves

1 Cut the rhubarb into 2.5 cm/1 in pieces. Place the rhubarb, water and lemon juice in a large, heavy-based pan and bring to the boil.

2 Peel and bruise the root ginger and add it to the pan. Simmer, stirring frequently, until the rhubarb is soft, then remove the ginger.

3 Add the sugar and stir until it has dissolved. Bring the mixture to the boil and boil rapidly for 10–15 minutes, or until setting point is reached. With a metal slotted spoon, remove any scum from the surface.

4 Add the preserved stem ginger and ginger mint leaves. Pour into warm, sterilized jars, cover and seal while the jam is hot and label when cold.

VARIATION: If ginger mint is not available you can substitute garden or apple mint. Avoid peppermint or Moroccan mint as these are more suitable for making mint tea.

COOK'S TIP: The early, forced rhubarb has the finest flavour.

Melon & Star Anise Jam

Melon and ginger are classic companions. The addition of star anise imparts a wonderful oriental flavour to the jam.

Makes 450 g/1 lb

INGREDIENTS
2 charentais or cantaloupe melons,
    peeled and seeded
450 g/1 lb/2¼ cups granulated (white) sugar
2 star anise
4 pieces preserved stem ginger in syrup,
    drained and finely chopped
finely grated rind (zest) and juice of
    2 lemons

1 Dice the melons and layer with the granulated sugar in a large non-metallic bowl. Cover with clear film (plastic wrap) and leave overnight so the melons can release their juices.

COOK'S TIP: The large amount of sugar is necessary for proper jelling. Use this jam in savoury dishes instead of honey to add a spicy, non-cloying sweetness.

2 Tip the marinated melons and their juice into a large, heavy-based pan and add the star anise, chopped preserved stem ginger, finely grated lemon rind and juice.

3 Bring to the boil over a medium heat, stirring to ensure that all the sugar has dissolved, then lower the heat. Simmer for 25 minutes, or until the melon has become transparent and the setting point has been reached. If preferred, remove the star anise, using a slotted spoon.

4 Spoon the jam into warm, sterilized jars. Cover the fruit with liquid and seal while it is hot and label when cold. It will keep for several months in a cool, dark cupboard. Once a jar has been opened, the jam should be stored in the refrigerator and used within 2 weeks.

Dried Apricot Jam

Make this jam when reserves of fresh fruit are low in winter.

Makes about 2 kg/4½ lb

INGREDIENTS
675 g/1½ lb dried apricots
900 ml/1½ pints/3¾ cups apple juice
juice and rind (zest) of 2 lemons
675 g/1½ lb/3½ cups granulated (white)
  sugar
50 g/2 oz/⅓ cup blanched almonds,
  coarsely chopped

1 Put the apricots in a large bowl and add the apple juice. Set aside to soak overnight.

2 Pour the apricots and juice into a pan and add the lemon juice and rind. Bring to the boil, lower the heat and simmer for 15–20 minutes.

3 Meanwhile, warm the sugar in a low oven. Add the warm sugar to the apricots and bring back to the boil, stirring constantly until the sugar has completely dissolved. Boil until setting point is reached.

4 Stir in the chopped almonds and set aside for 15 minutes. Pour the apricot jam into warm, sterilized jars. Cover and seal while the jam is hot and label when cold.

VARIATION: This recipe would also work well using dried peaches instead of the apricots.

Clementine Marmalade

Coriander seeds impart a warm and spicy flavour to this marmalade.

Makes about 2.75 kg/6 lb

INGREDIENTS
1.5 kg/3 lb clementines
6 lemons
30 ml/2 tbsp coriander seeds, roasted and
   roughly crushed
3 litres/5¼ pints/12 cups water
1.5 kg/3 lb/6¾ cups
   granulated (white) sugar

1 Cut the clementines and lemons in half. Squeeze all the fruit and pour the juice into a large, heavy-based pan.

2 Scrape the pith from the citrus shells and tie it, with the pips and half the coriander, in a piece of muslin. Add the bag to the juice.

3 Slice the clementine and lemon peels into fine shreds and add them to the pan with the water.

4 Bring the water to the boil, lower the heat and simmer for 1½ hours or until the peel is very soft. Remove the muslin bag. Holding it over the pan, squeeze it between two saucers.

5 Add the sugar and the remaining coriander to the pan and stir over a low heat until dissolved. Boil rapidly until setting point is reached. Skim the surface, then leave to stand for 30 minutes, stirring occasionally. Pour into warm, sterilized jars, cover and seal while the marmalade is hot and label when cold.

Three-fruit Marmalade

This zesty marmalade is incomparably better than store-bought varieties.

Makes 2.75 kg/6 lb

INGREDIENTS
350 g/12 oz oranges
350 g/12 oz lemons
675 g/1½ lb grapefruit
2.5 litres/4½ pints/10 cups water
2.75 kg/6 lb/14 cups granulated (white) sugar

3 Remove the fruit from the pan and cut it into quarters. Scrape out the pulp and add it to the pan with the cooking liquid.

1 Rinse and gently scrub the fruit with a vegetable brush.

2 Put all the fruit and water in a large, heavy-based saucepan. Add the water but make sure that it completely covers the fruit. Bring to the boil then simmer, uncovered, for 2 hours. Leave in the saucepan until the fruit is cool enough to be handled.

4 Cut the rinds into slivers and add to the pan. Add the sugar. Gently heat until the sugar has dissolved. Bring to the boil and cook until a setting point is reached. Leave to stand for 1 hour to allow the peel to settle.

5 Pour into warm, sterilized jars, cover and seal while the marmalade is hot and label when cold.

VARIATION: You can adjust the amount of orange or lemon in this recipe, keeping the same total weight, to produce a sweeter or tarter flavour.

16

Lemon & Lime Curd

Serve this creamy, tangy spread with toast or muffins, instead of jam, for a delightful change of flavour and texture.

Makes 900 g/2 lb

INGREDIENTS
115 g/4 oz/½ cup unsalted butter
3 eggs
2 lemons
2 limes
225 g/8 oz/1 cup caster (superfine) sugar

3 Finely grate the rinds (zest) of the lemons and limes, then cut them in half and squeeze the juice. Add the lemon and lime rinds and juices to the eggs and butter, then add the sugar.

1 Put the butter in a mixing bowl placed over a pan of simmering water, but not touching the surface.

4 Stir the mixture constantly until it thickens. Pour into small, warm sterilized jars. Cover and seal while the curd is hot and label when cold. The lemon and lime curd will keep unopened for up to a month. Once opened, keep in the refrigerator and consume within a week.

2 Lightly beat the eggs with a fork and add them to the butter.

Bramble Jelly

This jelly has to be made with hand-picked wild blackberries for the best flavour. Include a few red, unripe berries for a good set.

Makes 900 g/2 lb

INGREDIENTS
900 g/2 lb/8 cups blackberries
300 ml/½ pint/1¼ cups water
juice of 1 lemon
about 900 g/2 lb/4½ cups caster
  (superfine) sugar

3 Discard the fruit pulp. Measure the juice and allow 450 g/1 lb/2¼ cups sugar to every 600 ml/1 pint/2½ cups juice. Place the sugar and blackberry juice in a large, heavy-based pan and bring the mixture slowly to the boil, stirring constantly until the sugar has dissolved.

1 Put the blackberries, water and lemon juice into a large, heavy-based saucepan. Cover the pan and cook over a gentle heat for 15–30 minutes, or until the blackberries are very soft.

2 Ladle into a jelly bag or a large sieve lined with muslin and set over a large bowl. Leave to drip overnight to obtain the maximum amount of juice. Do not squeeze the bag as this will make the jelly cloudy.

4 Boil rapidly until setting point is reached. This will take about 10 minutes. Cool for 10 minutes. Skim off any scum and pour the jelly into warm, sterilized jars. Cover and seal while the jelly is hot and label the jars when cold.

VARIATION: Redcurrant jelly is made in the same way, but with less sugar. Reduce the quantity to 350 g/12 oz/1⅔ cups for every 600 ml/1 pint/2½ cups juice.

Crab Apple Jelly

Serve this jelly with game or use it to glaze an apple tart.

Makes about 1 kg/2¼ lb from each 600 ml/1 pint/ 2½ cups liquid

INGREDIENTS
1 kg/2¼ lb crab apples
3 cloves
900 g/2 lb/4½ cups granulated (white) sugar

1 Wash the apples and halve them, but do not peel or core. Place the apples and cloves in a large, heavy-based saucepan and cover with water. Bring to the boil, lower the heat and simmer until soft.

2 Ladle into a large jelly bag or a sieve lined with muslin and set over a large bowl. Leave to drain.

3 Warm the sugar in a low oven (120°C/250°F/Gas ½) for 15 minutes. Measure the juice and discard the fruit. Allow 450 g/1 lb/2¼ cups sugar for each 600 ml/1 pint/2½ cups of juice.

4 Put the juice and sugar in a large, heavy-based pan. Heat gently, stirring until the sugar dissolves, then boil rapidly until setting point is reached. Pour into warm, sterilized jars, cover and seal while the jelly is still hot and label when cold.

Rosehip & Apple Jelly

You can use windfall apples and rosehips from the hedgerows.

Makes about 1 kg/2¼ lb from each 600 ml/1 pint/ 2½ cups liquid

INGREDIENTS
1 kg/2¼ lb apples, peeled, trimmed
    and quartered
450 g/1 lb firm, ripe rosehips
450 g/1 lb/2 cups granulated (white) sugar

1 Put the apples in a large, heavy-based pan with just enough water to cover, plus 300 ml/½ pint/1¼ cups extra. Bring to the boil and cook the apples until they are a pulp. Coarsely chop the rosehips in a food processor. Add them to the pan and simmer for 10 minutes.

2 Leave to stand for 10 minutes, then ladle into a jelly bag or sieve lined with muslin and set over a bowl. Leave to drain overnight.

3 Measure the juice and discard the fruit. Allow 400 g/1 lb/2 cups sugar for each 600 ml/1 pint/2½ cups of liquid. Warm the sugar in a low oven. Bring the juice to the boil in a large, heavy-based pan and add the sugar. Stir until it has dissolved, then boil until setting point is reached. Pour into warm, sterilized jars, cover and seal while hot.

Rose Petal Jelly

This subtle jelly is ideal for traditional afternoon teas with thinly sliced bread and butter – it adds a real summer flavour.

Makes about 900 g/2 lb

INGREDIENTS
600 ml/1 pint/2½ cups red or
    pink roses
450 ml/¾ pint/scant 2 cups water
700 g/1 lb 9 oz/3½ cups caster
    (superfine) sugar
100 ml/3½ fl oz/scant ½ cup white
    grape juice
100 ml/3½ fl oz/scant ½ cup red
    grape juice
50 g/2 oz packet powdered
    fruit pectin
30 ml/2 tbsp rosewater

2 Strain the flowers from the syrup, and put the syrup in a large, heavy-based pan. Add the grape juices and pectin. Boil hard for 1 minute.

3 Add the remaining sugar and stir well. Boil the mixture hard for 1 minute more. Remove from the heat. Test for setting point – it should make a soft jelly, not a thick jam.

4 Finally, add the rosewater. Ladle the jelly into warm, sterilized jars, cover and seal while the jelly is hot and label when cold.

1 Carefully pull the rose petals away from the flower and trim them at the base to remove the white tips. Place the petals, water and about one-eighth of the sugar in a saucepan and bring to the boil. Reduce the heat and simmer for 5 minutes. Remove from the heat and leave to stand overnight for the rose fragrance to infuse.

COOK'S TIP: Powdered pectin is needed here because the jelly does not include fruit which contains its own pectin.

Jellies should be bright and clear and not too firmly set.

Mint & Apple Jelly

The vibrant flavour of this fresh mint-speckled jelly makes the perfect accompaniment to a delicious dinner of roast lamb.

Makes about 675 g/1½ lb

INGREDIENTS
1.5 kg/3 lb cooking apples
150 ml/¼ pint/⅔ cup cider vinegar
750 ml/1¼ pints/3 cups water
675 g/1½ lb/3½ cups granulated (white)
    sugar
60 ml/4 tbsp chopped fresh mint
few drops green food colouring (optional)

1 Roughly chop the apples, including cores and skin, and put into a large, heavy-based pan. Add the vinegar and water and bring to the boil. Reduce the heat and simmer for 30 minutes, or until the apples are pulpy.

2 Ladle the apple mixture into a jelly bag or sieve lined with muslin and set over a bowl. Drain for several hours.

3 Measure the juice and pour back into the pan. For every 600 ml/ 1 pint/2½ cups of juice, add 450 g/ 1 lb/2¼ cups sugar. Bring to the boil, stirring occasionally, until the sugar has completely dissolved.

4 Boil rapidly for 10–15 minutes, or until setting point is reached. Skim the jelly with a slotted spoon. Stir in the mint and a few drops of food colouring, if liked. Ladle into warm, sterilized jars, cover and seal while hot.

Apple & Strawberry Jelly

This versatile jelly is wonderful with sweet and savoury dishes and is delicious with both scones or roast pork or turkey.

Makes about 1 kg/2¼ lb

INGREDIENTS
900 g/2 lb cooking apples
1.2 litres/2 pints/5 cups water
900 g/2 lb strawberries
1 kg/2¼ lb/generous 5 cups
   granulated (white) sugar
5 stems rosemary

1 Chop the apples, including cores and skin, and put in a large heavy-based pan with the water. Bring to the boil and simmer for 15 minutes. Thickly slice the strawberries, add them to the pan, bring back to the boil and simmer for 15 minutes.

2 Ladle the fruit mixture into a large jelly bag or a sieve lined with muslin and set over a large bowl. Leave to drain for several hours or overnight.

3 Measure the juice and add 450 g/1 lb/2¼ cups sugar to every 600 ml/1 pint/2½ cups juice. Dissolve the sugar slowly then boil rapidly until setting point is reached.

4 Skim the jelly with a slotted spoon. Ladle it into warm, sterilized jars and leave to stand for about 10 minutes. Add a sprig of rosemary to each jar, cover and seal. Label the jars when cold.

Crab Apple & Lavender Jelly

This delicate, clear jelly with its fragrance of summer looks even prettier with a sprig of fresh lavender suspended in the jar.

Makes about 900 g/2 lb

INGREDIENTS
900 g/2 lb/5 cups crab apples
1.75 litres/3 pints/7½ cups water
lavender stems
900 g/2 lb/4½ cups granulated (white)
    sugar

1 Cut the unpeeled crab apples into chunks and place in a large, heavy-based pan with the water and 2 stems of lavender. Bring to the boil, cover and simmer very gently, stirring occasionally, for 1 hour, until the fruit is pulpy.

2 Pour the apple mixture into a large jelly bag or a sieve lined with muslin and set over a large bowl. Leave to drain for several hours or overnight. Do not squeeze the bag or the jelly will become cloudy.

3 Discard the crab apple pulp and measure the quantity of juice in the bowl. To each 600 ml/1 pint/2½ cups of juice add 450 g/1 lb/2¼ cups granulated sugar. Put the measured sugar and juice into a clean saucepan.

4 Heat the juice gently, stirring occasionally, until the sugar has dissolved. Bring to the boil and boil rapidly for about 8–10 minutes, until setting point has been reached. Remove the pan from the heat.

5 Skim the jelly with a slotted spoon. Ladle it into warm, sterilized jars. Dip the lavender stems quickly into boiling water, gently shake off the excess water, then insert a stem into each jar. Cover and seal while the jelly is hot and label the jars when cold.

Red Pepper & Rosemary Jelly

This wonderful amber-coloured jelly may be made with either red or yellow peppers and flavoured with any full-flavoured herbs.

Makes 1.75 kg/4 lb

INGREDIENTS
450 g/1 lb/8 tomatoes, quartered
4 red (bell) peppers, seeded and chopped
2 red chillies, seeded and chopped
rosemary sprigs, blanched in boiling water
300 ml/½ pint/1¼ cups water
300 ml/½ pint/1¼ cups red wine vinegar
2.5 ml/½ tsp salt
900 g/2 lb/4½ cups granulated (white) sugar
250 ml/8 fl oz/1 cup liquid pectin

1 Place the tomatoes, peppers, chillies, a few rosemary sprigs and the water into a large, heavy-based pan and bring to the boil. Cover and simmer for 1 hour, or until the peppers are tender and pulpy.

2 Ladle the mixture into a large jelly bag or a sieve lined with muslin and set over a large bowl. Leave to drain undisturbed for several hours or, preferably, overnight.

3 Place the juice in a clean saucepan with the vinegar, salt and sugar. Heat gently, stirring occasionally, until the sugar has dissolved. Boil rapidly for 3 minutes.

4 Remove the saucepan from the heat and stir in the liquid pectin. Skim the surface with a piece of kitchen paper to remove any foam.

5 Pour the liquid into warm, sterilized jars and add a sprig of rosemary to each jar. Cover and seal while hot and label when cold.

Fruit Preserves

The time to make these luxurious preserves is in high summer when the fruit is at its cheapest and most flavoursome. They are delicious served with cream or ice cream.

Brandied Peaches

Makes 1.75 kg/4 lb peaches, plus syrup

INGREDIENTS
1.75 kg/4 lb/10¼ cups caster
   (superfine) sugar
600 ml/1 pint/2½ cups water
2 cinnamon sticks, broken
15 ml/1 tbsp cloves
1.75 kg/4 lb ripe but firm peaches, scalded
   and peeled
400 ml/14 fl oz/1⅔ cups brandy

1 Dissolve the sugar in the water in a saucepan over a gentle heat. Tie the cinnamon sticks and cloves in a piece of muslin and add them to the sugar water. Bring to the boil.

2 Add the peaches, a few at a time, and simmer each batch for about 5 minutes, until just tender. Drain the cooked peaches, pouring the syrup back into the saucepan. When all the peaches are cooked, boil the syrup until it has thickened slightly. Cool for 10 minutes.

3 Stir the brandy into the syrup. Pack the peaches into hot, sterilized bottles, cover with the syrup and seal.

Cherries in Eau-de-vie

Makes 450 g/1 lb cherries, plus syrup

INGREDIENTS
450 g/1 lb/2⅔ cups ripe cherries
8 blanched almonds
90 ml/6 tbsp caster (superfine) sugar
550 ml/18 fl oz/2½ cups
   eau-de-vie

1 Wash and stone the cherries and then pack them, together with the blanched almonds, into a sterilized, wide-necked bottle.

2 Spoon the sugar evenly over the cherries and almonds, then add the eau-de-vie so that the cherries are completely covered. Seal the top securely.

3 Store in a cool, dark place for 1 month before using the cherries, shaking the bottle from time to time to help dissolve the sugar.

COOK'S TIP: Whole, preserved cherries can also be dipped in melted chocolate.

Poached Spiced Plums in Brandy

Makes 900 g/2 lb

INGREDIENTS
600 ml/1 pint/2½ cups brandy
rind (zest) of 1 lemon, peeled in a long strip
350 g/12 oz/1⅔ cups caster (superfine) sugar
1 cinnamon stick
900 g/2 lb fresh plums

1 Put the brandy, lemon rind, sugar and cinnamon stick in a large saucepan and heat gently to dissolve the sugar. Add the plums and poach for about 15 minutes, or until soft. Remove with a slotted spoon.

2 Reduce the syrup by a third by rapid boiling. Strain it over the plums. Bottle the plums in large sterilized jars. Seal tightly and store for up to 6 months in a cool, dark place.

COOK'S TIP: This recipe would also work well with golden plums or damsons. For an extra fruity flavour, you could use plum brandy, quetsch or prunella, and mirabelle would be ideal for golden plums.

Above: Poached Spiced Plums in Brandy

33

Candied Citrus Slices

To preserve the individual flavour of each citrus fruit they should all be candied separately.

Makes about 675 g/1½ lb

INGREDIENTS
5 large oranges or 10 lemons
    or 10 limes
675 g/1½ lb/3½ cups caster (superfine) sugar,
    plus extra for sprinkling
250 ml/8 fl oz/1 cup cold water

1 Halve the fruit, squeeze out the juice and discard the flesh, but retain the pith.

2 Cut the peel into strips about 1 cm/½ in wide and place them in a pan. Cover with boiling water and simmer for 5 minutes. Drain and then repeat this process 4 times, using fresh boiling water each time, to remove the peel's bitterness.

3 Put the sugar in a heavy-based pan and pour in the cold water. Heat gently to dissolve the sugar. Add the peel, partially cover and simmer over a low heat for 30–40 minutes, until soft. Leave to cool completely, then sprinkle with sugar to thoroughly cover the peel. Store the candied peel in an airtight container for up to 1 year.

Right: Candied Citrus Slices

Candied Ginger

You can use candied ginger in your cakes and puddings or simply nibble a piece as a treat.

Makes about 675 g/1½ lb

INGREDIENTS
350 g/12 oz fresh root ginger
225 g/8 oz/1 cup caster (superfine) sugar,
    plus extra for coating
120 ml/4 fl oz/½ cup water

1 Place the ginger in a saucepan and cover with water. Bring to the boil and simmer for 15 minutes. Drain and leave to cool. Peel the ginger and cut it into 5 mm/¼ in slices.

2 Place the sugar and water in a heavy-based saucepan. Heat gently until the sugar has dissolved, then simmer without stirring, for about 15 minutes or until the mixture is syrupy.

3 Add the ginger and cook over a low heat, shaking the pan occasionally until the syrup has been absorbed. Remove the ginger slices from the pan and place them on a wire rack to cool.

4 Coat the slices with caster sugar and spread them out on greaseproof (waxed) paper for 2–3 days, until the sugar has crystallized. Stored in an airtight jar, they will keep indefinitely.

Fruits in Liqueur

Choose from apricots, clementines, kumquats, physalis, cherries, strawberries, raspberries, peaches, plums, star fruit or seedless grapes and team them with rum, brandy, kirsch or Cointreau.

Makes 450 g/1 lb

INGREDIENTS
450 g/1 lb/3 cups fresh fruit
225 g/8 oz/generous 1 cup caster (superfine) sugar
300 ml/½ pint/1¼ cups water
150 ml/¼ pint/⅔ cup liqueur or spirit

1 Wash the fruit. Halve and stone apricots, plums or peaches. Slice star fruit, remove the husk from physalis, hull strawberries or raspberries, and prick kumquats, cherries or grapes all over with a cocktail stick. Pare the rind from clementines using a sharp knife, taking care not to include any white pith.

2 Place 115 g/4 oz/scant ½ cup of the sugar and the water into a saucepan. Heat gently, stirring occasionally, until the sugar has dissolved. Bring to the boil.

3 Add the fruit and simmer gently for 1–2 minutes, until the fruit is just tender, but the skins are intact and the fruits are whole.

4 Carefully remove the fruit using a slotted spoon and arrange neatly in warm, sterilized jars. Add the remaining sugar to the syrup in the pan and stir until dissolved.

5 Boil the syrup rapidly until it reaches 107°C/225°F or the thread stage. Test by pressing a small amount of syrup between 2 teaspoons; when they are pulled apart, a thread should form. Allow to cool.

6 Measure the cooled syrup, then add an equal quantity of liqueur or spirit. Mix until blended. Pour over the fruit until covered. Seal each jar and keep for up to 4 months.

Raspberry Preserve

The wonderfully fresh flavour of this fruit preserve makes it a welcome gift if you can bear to part with it.

Makes 900 g/2 lb

INGREDIENTS
675 g/1½ lb/4 cups raspberries
900 g/2 lb/4½ cups caster
   (superfine) sugar
30 ml/2 tbsp lemon juice
120 ml/4 fl oz/½ cup
   liquid pectin

1 Place the raspberries in a large bowl and lightly crush with a wooden spoon. Stir in the caster sugar. Leave for 1 hour at room temperature, stirring occasionally.

2 Add the lemon juice and pectin to the raspberries and stir until thoroughly blended.

3 Spoon the raspberry mixture into sterilized jars, leaving a 1 cm/½ in space at the top if the jam is to be frozen. Cover the surface of each with a greaseproof (waxed) paper disc and seal with a lid or cellophane paper and an elastic band. Do not use a screw-topped lid if the jam is to be frozen. Label and freeze for up to 6 months, or refrigerate for up to 4 weeks.

Traditional Mincemeat

Mince pies are an essential part of the traditional Christmas fare, enjoyed in considerable quantities throughout the holiday.

Makes about 1.75 g/4 lb

INGREDIENTS
450 g/1 lb cooking apples
225 g/8 oz/1½ cups candied citrus peel
225 g/8 oz/1 cup currants
225 g/8 oz/1⅓ cups sultanas (golden raisins)
450 g/1 lb/3¼ cups seedless raisins
115 g/4 oz/⅔ cup blanched almonds, chopped
225 g/8 oz/1⅔ cup suet or vegetarian suet
225 g/8 oz/1 cup dark brown sugar
5 ml/1 tsp ground cinnamon
5 ml/1 tsp ground allspice
5 ml/1 tsp ground ginger
2.5 ml/½ tsp grated nutmeg
grated rind and juice of 2 oranges
grated rind and juice of 2 lemons
about 150 ml/¼ pint/⅔ cup brandy or port

1 Peel, core and chop the cooking apples. Chop the candied citrus peel.

2 Place all the ingredients, except the brandy or port, in a large mixing bowl. Stir well.

3 Cover the bowl with a cloth and set aside in a cool place overnight for the fruit to swell.

4 The following day, stir in enough brandy or port to make a mixture moist enough to drop from a spoon.

5 Spoon the mixture into sterilized jars and cover and store in a cool, dry place.

Mediterranean Marinated Peppers with Spices

Highly decorative and fragrantly delicious, these peppers can be used as part of a mixed platter of appetizers.

Makes 1kg/2¼ lb

INGREDIENTS
1 kg/2¼ lb mixed red, yellow and
   orange (bell) peppers
550 ml/18 fl oz/2½ cups extra virgin
   olive oil
2 garlic cloves, sliced
1 cinnamon stick, halved
2.5 ml/½ tsp black peppercorns
6 cloves
6 dried red chillies

1 Preheat the grill (broiler) to hot. Halve, core and seed the peppers and cut into chunky pieces. Put them, skin side up, on a baking sheet. Brush with a little of the oil, then grill (broil) until the skins are blackened. Do not overcook or the flesh will be too soft. Cover with a dish towel or place in a bowl and cover with clear film (plastic wrap) and leave to cool.

2 Put the garlic, cinnamon stick and remaining spices into a saucepan with a little of the oil. Fry for a minute, add the remaining oil and bring to the boil.

3 Meanwhile, peel the skins off the peppers with a small, sharp knife and pack the pepper strips into warm, sterilized jars.

4 Allow the oil and spice mixture to cool, then pour it over the peppers, making sure the oil covers them completely. Seal the jars with screw-topped lids and label.

COOK'S TIP: Keep in an airtight container in the refrigerator for up to 3 weeks. Bring back to room temperature before serving.

Spiced Pickled Pears

These delicious and unusual pears are the perfect accompaniment for cooked ham or cold meat salads.

Makes 900 g/2 lb

INGREDIENTS
900 g/2 lb pears
600 ml/1 pint/2½ cups white wine vinegar
225 g/8 oz/1 cup caster (superfine) sugar
1 cinnamon stick
5 star anise
10 whole cloves

1 Peel the pears, keeping them whole and leaving on the stalks. Heat the vinegar and sugar together until the sugar has dissolved. Add the pears to the pan and poach for 15 minutes.

2 Add the cinnamon stick, star anise and whole cloves and simmer for 10 minutes. Remove the cooked pears and pack tightly into warm, sterilized jars. Simmer the syrup for a further 15 minutes and pour it over the pears, making sure it covers them completely.

3 Seal the jars tightly while still hot and label when cold. Store in a cool, dark place. The spiced pears will keep for up to a year unopened. Once opened, store in the refrigerator and consume within a week.

Dill Pickles

A good pickle to have in your store cupboard. It is excellent sliced in hamburgers, served with cold meats, or in canapés and snacks.

Makes about 2.4 litres/4 pints

INGREDIENTS
6 small cucumbers, or 6 large or
    12 small gherkins
475 ml/16 fl oz/2 cups
    water
1 litre/1¾ pints/4 cups white
    wine vinegar
115 g/4 oz/½ cup salt
3 bay leaves
45 ml/3 tbsp dill seed
2 garlic cloves, slivered

1 Slice the cucumbers into medium-thick slices. If using small gherkins leave whole or slice lengthways. Put the water, vinegar and salt in a saucepan and bring to the boil, then remove immediately from the heat.

2 Layer the herbs and garlic between slices of cucumber or gherkins in warm, sterilized preserving jars until the jars are full, then cover with the warm salt and vinegar mixture. Seal and leave on a sunny windowsill for at least a week before using.

Mellow Golden Apple & Tomato Chutney

This golden, spicy chutney transforms a ploughman's lunch and goes well with cold roast chicken.

Makes about 3 kh/6 lb

INGREDIENTS

1.5 kg/3 lb cooking apples, peeled
1.5 kg/3 lb tomatoes, skins removed
2 large onions
2 garlic cloves
250 g/9 oz/1¼ cups stoned (pitted) dates
2 red (bell) peppers
3 dried red chillies
15 ml/1 tbsp black peppercorns
4 cardamom pods
15 ml/1 tbsp coriander seeds
10 ml/2 tsp cumin seeds
10 ml/2 tsp turmeric
15 ml/1 tbsp salt
600 ml/1 pint/2½ cups distilled malt vinegar
1 kg/2¼ lb/generous 5 cups preserving sugar

1 Quarter, core and chop the apples. Chop the tomatoes, onions and garlic. Quarter the dates. Core and seed the peppers, then cut into chunks.

2 Put all the prepared ingredients, except the red peppers, into a large, heavy-based pan.

3 Slit the chillies. Put them with the peppercorns and remaining spices into a mortar and roughly crush with a pestle. Add all the prepared spices, turmeric and salt to the pan.

4 Pour in the vinegar and sugar and bring to the boil, stirring. Simmer for 30 minutes, stirring occasionally. Add the red pepper and cook for a further 30 minutes, stirring more frequently as the chutney becomes thick and pulpy.

5 Spoon into warm, sterilized jars. Cover and seal while the chutney is hot and label when cold. Leave for two weeks before tasting. Store unopened jars for up to a year in a cool, dark place.

Christmas Chutney

This savoury mixture of spices and dried fruit takes its inspiration from traditional mincemeat.

Makes 900 g–1.5 kg/2–3 lb

INGREDIENTS
450 g/1 lb cooking apples, peeled, cored and chopped
500 g/1¼ lb/3 cups good quality mixed dried fruit
grated rind of 1 orange
30 ml/2 tbsp mixed (apple pie) spice
150 ml/¼ pint/⅔ cup cider vinegar
350 g/12 oz/1½ cups light brown sugar

1 Place the apples, dried fruit and orange rind in a large, heavy-based saucepan. Stir in the mixed spice, vinegar and sugar. Heat gently, stirring until all the sugar has dissolved.

2 Bring to the boil, then lower the heat and simmer, stirring occasionally, for 40–45 minutes, until the mixture is thick. Ladle into warm, sterilized jars. Cover and seal while the chutney is hot and label when cold. Keep for 1 month before using.

COOK'S TIP: Watch the chutney carefully towards the end of the cooking time as it has a tendency to catch on the bottom of the pan. Stir frequently at this stage.

Green Tomato Chutney

This is a classic chutney to make at the end of summer to use up the last unripened tomatoes.

Makes about 2.5 kg/5½ lb

INGREDIENTS
1.75 kg/4 lb green tomatoes, roughly chopped
450 g/1 lb cooking apples, peeled, cored and chopped
450 g/1 lb onions, chopped
2 large garlic cloves, crushed
15 ml/1 tbsp salt
45 ml/3 tbsp pickling spice
600 ml/1 pint/2½ cups cider vinegar
450 g/1 lb/2¼ cups preserving sugar

1 Place the tomatoes, apples, onions and garlic in a large saucepan. Add the salt. Tie the pickling spice in a piece of muslin and add to the pan.

2 Pour in half the vinegar and bring to the boil. Lower the heat and simmer, stirring frequently, for 1 hour.

3 Dissolve the sugar in the remaining vinegar and add to the chutney. Simmer, stirring often, for 1½ hours. Remove the muslin bag. Spoon the hot chutney into warm, sterilized jars. Cover and seal while hot.

Right: Christmas Chutney (top); Green Tomato Chutney

Fig & Date Chutney

This recipe is usually made with dried figs and dates, but it works perfectly well with fresh fruit and has a superb flavour.

Makes 450 g/1 lb

INGREDIENTS
1 orange
5 large fresh figs, coarsely chopped
350 g/12 oz/2 cups fresh dates, peeled,
    stoned and chopped
2 onions, chopped
5 cm/2 in piece of fresh root ginger, peeled
    and finely grated
5 ml/1 tsp dried crushed chillies
300 g/11 oz/1½ cups preserving sugar
300 ml/½ pint/1¼ cups spiced
    preserving vinegar
2.5 ml/½ tsp salt

1 Finely grate the rind (zest) of the orange, then cut off the remaining pith and segment the orange.

COOK'S TIP: If using dried figs and dates increase the amount of spiced preserving vinegar to 450 ml/¾ pint/scant 2 cups.

2 Place the orange segments in a large, heavy-based saucepan with the chopped fresh figs and dates. Add the orange rind, then stir in the chopped onions, grated ginger, crushed chillies, sugar, preserving vinegar and salt. Gradually bring to the boil, stirring gently, until all the sugar has dissolved.

3 Lower the heat and simmer gently, stirring often to prevent the mixture from sticking to the base of the pan, for 1 hour, or until the mixture has thickened and become pulpy in texture.

4 Spoon the chutney into warm, sterilized jars. Seal while hot and label when the chutney is cold. Store for a week before using, to allow the flavours to develop. Once a jar has been opened, keep it in the refrigerator. Store unopened jars in a dry, dark cupboard for up to 1 year.

Windfall Pear Chutney

A tasty way to use those hard windfall pears.

Makes about 2 kg/5 lb

INGREDIENTS
675 g/1½ lb pears, peeled, cored
   and chopped
225 g/8 oz onions, chopped
175 g/6 oz/generous 1 cup raisins
115 g/4 oz apples, cored and chopped
60 ml/4 tbsp chopped preserved stem ginger
115 g/4 oz/1 cup walnuts, chopped
1 garlic clove, chopped
juice and rind of 1 lemon
600 ml/1 pint/2½ cups cider vinegar
175 g/6 oz/¾ cup brown sugar
2 cloves
5 ml/1 tsp salt

1 Place the pears, onions, raisins, apples, ginger, walnuts, garlic and lemon juice and rind in a non-metallic bowl. Put the vinegar, sugar, cloves and salt into a saucepan. Stir over a low heat until the sugar has dissolved. Bring to the boil and pour over the pear mixture. Cover and leave overnight for the flavours to develop.

2 Next day, transfer the pear mixture to a large, heavy-based pan. Bring to the boil and simmer for 1½ hours, until soft and thickened. Spoon into warm, sterilized jars. Cover and seal while the chutney is hot.

Kashmir Chutney

A typical family recipe passed down through the generations.

Makes about 2.75 kg/6 lb

INGREDIENTS
1 kg/2¼ lb green apples
2-3 garlic cloves
1 litre/1¾ pints/4 cups malt vinegar
450 g/1 lb/2⅔ cups dates, stoned
115 g/4 oz preserved stem ginger
450 g/1 lb/3¼ cups
   seeded raisins
450 g/1 lb/2¼ cups
   brown sugar
2.5 ml/½ tsp cayenne pepper
30 ml/2 tbsp salt

1 Quarter the apples, without peeling them, remove the cores and chop coarsely. Peel and chop the garlic.

2 Place the apples and garlic in a saucepan with enough vinegar to cover and boil until soft. Chop the dates and ginger and add them to the cooked apple and garlic together with all the other ingredients.

3 Boil gently for 45 minutes. Spoon the mixture into warm, sterilized jars. Cover and seal while the chutney is hot and label the jars when cold.

Right: Kashmir Chutney (left);
Windfall Pear Chutney

Mango Chutney

This classic chutney is conventionally served with curries and Indian poppadums, but it is also delicious with baked ham or a traditional ploughman's lunch as a change from tomato chutney.

Makes 450 g/1 lb

INGREDIENTS
3 firm green mangoes
150 ml/¼ pint/⅔ cup cider vinegar
130 g/4½ oz/generous ½ cup light
   muscovado sugar
1 small red finger chilli or
   jalapeño chilli, split
2.5 cm/1 in piece of fresh
   root ginger, peeled and
   finely chopped
1 garlic clove, finely chopped
5 cardamom pods, bruised
2.5 ml/½ tsp coriander
   seeds, crushed
1 bay leaf
2.5 ml/½ tsp salt

1 Peel the mangoes and cut the flesh off the stones. Slice the mangoes lengthways, then cut across into small chunks or thin wedges.

2 Place the mango pieces in a large saucepan, add the cider vinegar and cover. Cook the mixture over a low heat for 10 minutes.

3 Stir in the muscovado sugar, split chilli, chopped ginger and garlic, bruised cardamom pods and crushed coriander seeds. Add the bay leaf and salt. Bring to the boil slowly, stirring often to prevent the chutney sticking to the base of the saucepan.

4 Lower the heat and simmer, uncovered, for 30 minutes, or until the mixture is thick and pulpy.

5 Ladle into warm, sterilized jars. Cover and seal while the chutney is hot and label when cold. Store for 1 week before eating. Keep in the refrigerator after opening.

Pickled Peach Chutney

This is a spicy, rich chutney that is great served with a strongly-flavoured farmhouse Cheddar.

Makes 450 g/1 lb

INGREDIENTS
475 ml/16 fl oz/2 cups cider vinegar
275 g/10 oz/1¼ cups light muscovado sugar
225 g/8 oz/1 cup dried dates, stoned and finely chopped
5 ml/1 tsp ground allspice
5 ml/1 tsp ground mace
450 g/1 lb ripe peaches, stoned and cut into small chunks
3 onions, thinly sliced
4 fresh red chillies, seeded and finely chopped
4 garlic cloves, crushed
5 cm/2 in piece of fresh root ginger, finely grated
5 ml/1 tsp salt

1 Place the vinegar, sugar, dates and spices in a large, heavy-based saucepan and bring to the boil, stirring occasionally. Add all the remaining ingredients and return to the boil. Lower the heat and simmer for 40–50 minutes, or until thick, stirring often.

2 Spoon into warm, sterilized jars. Cover and seal while the chutney is hot. Store in the refrigerator and use within 2 months.

Nectarine Relish

This sweet and tangy fruit relish goes very well with hot roast meats and game birds.

Makes 450g/1 lb

INGREDIENTS
45 ml/3 tbsp olive oil
2 Spanish onions, thinly sliced
1 fresh green chilli, seeded and finely chopped
5 ml/1 tsp fresh rosemary, finely chopped
2 bay leaves
450 g/1 lb nectarines, stoned and cut into chunks
150 g/5 oz/1 cup raisins
10 ml/2 tsp crushed coriander seeds
350 g/12 oz/1½ cups demerara sugar
200 ml/7 fl oz/scant 1 cup red wine vinegar

1 Heat the oil in a large, heavy-based pan. Add the onions, chilli, rosemary and bay leaves. Cook, stirring often, for 15–20 minutes.

2 Add all the remaining ingredients and bring to the boil over a low heat, stirring often. Simmer, stirring occasionally, for 1 hour.

3 Spoon into warm, sterilized jars. Cover and seal while the chutney is hot and label when cold. Store in the refrigerator for up to 5 months.

Right: Nectarine Relish (top);
Pickled Peach Chutney

Bread & Butter Pickles

This is a traditional American pickle with a distinctive blend of whole spices.

Makes about 1.75 kg/4 lb

INGREDIENTS
900 g/2 lb cucumbers, cut into
    5 mm/¼ in slices
2 onions, thinly sliced
50 g/2 oz/¼ cup salt
350 ml/12 fl oz/1½ cups cider vinegar
350 g/12 oz/1⅔ cups
    preserving sugar
30 ml/2 tbsp white mustard seeds
10 ml/2 tsp celery seeds
2.5 ml/½ tsp ground turmeric
2.5 ml/½ tsp black peppercorns

1 Put the cucumbers and onions in a large bowl. Mix in the salt. Fit a plate inside the bowl, pressing down on the cucumber mixture. Add a weight and leave for 3 hours. Drain the cucumber mixture, rinse under cold running water and drain again.

2 Put the remaining ingredients in a large saucepan. Bring to the boil, stirring to dissolve the sugar. Add the cucumber and onions. Bring to the boil, then remove the pan from the heat. Spoon the pickle into warm, sterilized jars. Cover and seal while the pickles are hot. Store for 1 month before using.

Fresh Tomato & Onion Chutney

Indian chutneys of this type are not meant to be kept, but are eaten when freshly made.

Serves 4–6

INGREDIENTS
2 tomatoes, finely diced
1 red onion, finely diced
1 fresh green chilli, seeded and chopped
60 ml/4 tbsp chopped fresh coriander
    (cilantro)
juice of 1 lime
2.5 ml/½ tsp salt
2.5 ml/½ tsp ground paprika
2.5 ml/½ tsp cayenne pepper
2.5 ml/½ tsp cumin seeds, roasted and
    ground

1 Place the diced tomatoes and onion in a bowl. Add the remaining ingredients to the bowl. Mix well and serve as soon as possible to enjoy its fresh taste.

Right: Bread & Butter Pickles (left); Fresh Tomato & Onion Chutney

Toffee Onion Relish

This melt-in-the-mouth caramelized relish is excellent partnered with grilled goat's cheese as a tasty lunchtime snack.

Serves 4

INGREDIENTS
3 large onions
50 g/2 oz/4 tbsp butter
30 ml/2 tbsp olive oil
30 ml/2 tbsp light muscovado sugar
30 ml/2 tbsp pickled capers
30 ml/2 tbsp chopped
    fresh parsley
salt and freshly ground
    black pepper

1 Peel the onions and halve them vertically through the core, then slice them thinly.

2 Heat the butter and olive oil together in a large saucepan. Add the sliced onions and muscovado sugar and cook very gently over a low heat, stirring occasionally, for 30 minutes, until reduced to a soft, rich brown toffee-like mixture.

3 Roughly chop the capers and stir into the toffee onions. Allow the mixture to cool completely.

4 Stir in the chopped fresh parsley and season with salt and pepper to taste. Cover the relish and chill until ready to serve.

VARIATION: Try making this recipe with red onions or shallots for a subtle variation in flavour.

Piccalilli

The piquancy of this traditional relish partners well with cold meats.

Makes 1.5 kg/3 lb

INGREDIENTS
675 g/1½ lb cauliflower
450 g/1 lb small onions
350 g/12 oz green beans
10 ml/2 tsp ground turmeric
10 ml/2 tsp dry mustard powder
10 ml/2 tsp cornflour (cornstarch)
600 ml/1 pint/2½ cups vinegar

3 Put the turmeric, mustard powder and cornflour into a small saucepan and pour over the vinegar. Stir well and simmer for 10 minutes.

1 Using a sharp knife, cut the cauliflower into tiny florets, removing the stalks.

4 Put the prepared vegetables into a large, heavy-based pan. Pour the vinegar mixture over the vegetables, mix well and simmer for 45 minutes.

2 Peel the onions, then top and tail the green beans and cut them into 2.5 cm/1 in lengths.

5 Pour into warm, sterilized jars. Cover and seal while the relish is hot and label when cold. Store in a cool dark place. The piccalilli will keep unopened for up to a year. Once opened, store in the refrigerator and consume within a week.

Moutarde aux Fines Herbes

This classic, fragrant mustard may be used as a condiment or for coating chicken, pork or oily fish before cooking.

Makes 300 ml/½ pint

INGREDIENTS
75 g/3 oz white mustard seeds
50 g/2 oz/¼ cup light brown sugar
5 ml/1 tsp salt
5 ml/1 tsp whole peppercorns
2.5 ml/½ tsp turmeric
200 ml/7 fl oz/scant 1 cup distilled
    malt vinegar
60 ml/4 tbsp chopped fresh mixed herbs,
    such as parsley, sage, thyme and rosemary

1 Put the mustard seeds, sugar, salt, peppercorns and turmeric into a blender or food processor and process.

2 Gradually add the vinegar, 15 ml/ 1 tbsp at a time, processing well between each addition, then continue processing until a coarse paste forms. Add the fresh herbs and mix well.

3 Leave to stand for 10–15 minutes to thicken slightly. Spoon into a 300 ml/½ pint/1¼ cup jar or several smaller jars, using a funnel. Cover the surface of the mustard with a waxed paper disc, then seal with a screw-topped lid or a cork, and label.

Clove-spiced Mustard

This spicy mustard is the perfect accompaniment to sausages and steaks, particularly when they are barbecued.

Makes 300 ml/½ pint

INGREDIENTS
75 g/3 oz white mustard seeds
50 g/2 oz/¼ cup light brown sugar
5 ml/1 tsp salt
5 ml/1 tsp black peppercorns
5 ml/1 tsp cloves
5 ml/1 tsp turmeric
200 ml/7 fl oz/1 cup distilled malt vinegar

1 Put all the ingredients except the vinegar into a blender or food processor and process.

2 Gradually add the vinegar, 15 ml/ 1 tbsp at a time, processing well between each addition, then continue processing until a coarse paste forms.

3 Leave to stand for 10–15 minutes to thicken slightly. Spoon into a 300 ml/½ pint/1¼ cup jar or several smaller jars, using a funnel. Cover the surface of the mustard with a waxed paper disc, then seal with a screw-topped lid or a cork, and label.

Right: Moutarde aux Fines Herbes (left); Clove-spiced Mustard

Index

This edition is published by Lorenz Books,
an imprint of Anness Publishing Ltd,
108 Great Russell Street, London WC1B 3NA info@anness.com
www.lorenzbooks.com; www.annesspublishing.com

© Anness Publishing Limited 2014

If you like the images in this book and would like to investigate using them for publishing, promotions or advertising, please visit our website www.practicalpictures.com for more information.

Publisher: Joanna Lorenz
Editor: Valerie Ferguson & Helen Sudell
Designer: Andrew Heath
Production Controller: Steve Lang

Recipes contributed by: Stephanie Donaldson,
Silvano Franco, Sara Lewis, Lesley Mackley,
Maggie Mayhew, Janice Murfitt, Katherine Richmond,
Liz Trigg, Pamela Westland.

Photography: William Adams-Lingwood,
Edward Allwright, John Freeman, Michelle Garrett, Nelson
Hargreaves, Polly Wreford.

A CIP catalogue record for this book is available from the British Library

COOK'S NOTES

Bracketed terms are intended for American readers.

For all recipes, quantities are given in both metric and imperial measures and, where appropriate, in standard cups and spoons. Follow one set of measures, but not a mixture, because they are not interchangeable.

Standard spoon and cup measures are level. 1 tsp = 5ml, 1 tbsp = 15ml, 1 cup = 250ml/8fl oz. Australian standard tablespoons are 20ml. Australian readers should use 3 tsp in place of 1 tbsp for measuring small quantities.

American pints are 16fl oz/2 cups. American readers should use 20fl oz/2.5 cups in place of 1 pint when measuring liquids.

Electric oven temperatures in this book are for conventional ovens. When using a fan oven, the temperature will probably need to be reduced by about 10–20°C/20–40°F. Since ovens vary, you should check with your manufacturer's instruction book for guidance.

Medium (US large) eggs are used unless otherwise stated.

PUBLISHER'S NOTE:

Although the advice and information in this book are believed to be accurate and true at the time of going to press, neither the authors nor the publisher can accept any legal responsibility or liability for any errors or omissions that may have been made nor for any inaccuracies nor for any loss, harm or injury that comes about from following instructions or advice in this book.